50 Low-Sodium Cooking Recipes for Home

By: Kelly Johnson

Table of Contents

- Low-Sodium Vegetable Soup
- Baked Lemon Herb Chicken
- Grilled Salmon with Herbed Quinoa
- Roasted Garlic and Rosemary Pork Tenderloin
- Lemon Garlic Shrimp Stir-Fry
- Herb-Roasted Turkey Breast
- Baked Cod with Mediterranean Vegetables
- Quinoa and Black Bean Stuffed Peppers
- Turkey Meatball and Vegetable Soup
- Grilled Chicken Caesar Salad
- Broiled Tilapia with Lemon-Dill Sauce
- Roasted Vegetable and Chickpea Salad
- Low-Sodium Beef and Vegetable Stir-Fry
- Herbed Roast Beef with Red Wine Reduction
- Lemon Herb Baked Chicken Thighs
- Eggplant and Tomato Gratin
- Grilled Portobello Mushrooms with Balsamic Glaze
- Low-Sodium Minestrone Soup
- Baked Lemon Pepper Chicken Breasts
- Spaghetti Squash with Marinara Sauce
- Turkey and Vegetable Stir-Fry
- Poached Salmon with Dill Sauce
- Low-Sodium Chicken and Vegetable Curry
- Roasted Brussels Sprouts with Garlic and Parmesan
- Herb-Crusted Pork Chops
- Lemon Garlic Roasted Chicken Drumsticks
- Grilled Vegetable and Quinoa Salad
- Low-Sodium Beef and Barley Soup
- Lemon Herb Baked Cod
- Turkey and Quinoa Stuffed Bell Peppers
- Baked Chicken Parmesan
- Roasted Asparagus with Lemon Zest
- Low-Sodium Chicken Fajitas
- Herb-Marinated Grilled Steak
- Lemon Herb Roasted Turkey Breast

- Low-Sodium Lentil Soup
- Grilled Lemon Garlic Shrimp Skewers
- Roasted Cauliflower with Garlic and Herbs
- Low-Sodium Vegetable and Bean Chili
- Baked Lemon Herb Tilapia
- Turkey and Vegetable Skillet
- Herb-Roasted Chicken Thighs
- Lemon Garlic Roasted Salmon
- Low-Sodium Beef and Broccoli Stir-Fry
- Quinoa Salad with Lemon Herb Vinaigrette
- Grilled Vegetable and Hummus Wrap
- Low-Sodium Chicken and Rice Casserole
- Herb-Marinated Grilled Chicken Breast
- Lemon Herb Baked Halibut
- Low-Sodium Ratatouille

Low-Sodium Vegetable Soup

Ingredients:

- 2 tablespoons olive oil
- 1 onion, diced
- 2 carrots, diced
- 2 stalks celery, diced
- 2 cloves garlic, minced
- 1 zucchini, diced
- 1 yellow squash, diced
- 1 bell pepper, diced
- 1 can (14 oz) diced tomatoes, undrained
- 6 cups low-sodium vegetable broth
- 1 teaspoon dried thyme
- 1 teaspoon dried oregano
- Salt and pepper to taste
- Fresh parsley or basil for garnish (optional)

Instructions:

Heat the olive oil in a large pot or Dutch oven over medium heat.
Add the diced onion, carrots, and celery to the pot. Cook, stirring occasionally, until the vegetables start to soften, about 5-7 minutes.
Add the minced garlic to the pot and cook for another 1-2 minutes until fragrant.
Stir in the diced zucchini, yellow squash, and bell pepper. Cook for another 5 minutes, stirring occasionally.
Add the diced tomatoes (with their juices) to the pot, along with the low-sodium vegetable broth, dried thyme, and dried oregano. Season with salt and pepper to taste.
Bring the soup to a simmer and let it cook for about 15-20 minutes, or until all the vegetables are tender.
Taste the soup and adjust the seasoning with more salt and pepper if needed.
Serve the low-sodium vegetable soup hot, garnished with fresh parsley or basil if desired.

This soup is packed with flavorful and nutritious vegetables, making it a healthy and satisfying option for lunch or dinner. It's also versatile, so feel free to add any other vegetables or herbs you have on hand. Enjoy!

Baked Lemon Herb Chicken

Ingredients:

- 4 boneless, skinless chicken breasts
- 2 tablespoons olive oil
- 2 cloves garlic, minced
- 2 teaspoons dried thyme
- 2 teaspoons dried rosemary
- 1 teaspoon dried oregano
- Zest of 1 lemon
- Juice of 1 lemon
- Salt and pepper to taste
- Fresh parsley, chopped (for garnish, optional)

Instructions:

Preheat your oven to 375°F (190°C).

In a small bowl, mix together the olive oil, minced garlic, dried thyme, dried rosemary, dried oregano, lemon zest, lemon juice, salt, and pepper.

Place the chicken breasts in a baking dish or oven-safe skillet.

Pour the lemon herb mixture over the chicken breasts, making sure to coat them evenly.

Bake the chicken in the preheated oven for 25-30 minutes, or until the chicken is cooked through and no longer pink in the center. The internal temperature should reach 165°F (74°C).

Once the chicken is cooked, remove it from the oven and let it rest for a few minutes.

Garnish the baked lemon herb chicken with chopped fresh parsley, if desired, before serving.

Serve the chicken hot with your favorite sides, such as roasted vegetables, rice, or salad.

This baked lemon herb chicken is flavorful, tender, and perfect for a quick and easy weeknight dinner. Enjoy the bright and zesty flavors of lemon and herbs!

Grilled Salmon with Herbed Quinoa

Ingredients:

For the Grilled Salmon:

- 4 salmon fillets, skin-on or skinless
- 2 tablespoons olive oil
- 2 cloves garlic, minced
- 1 teaspoon lemon zest
- 2 tablespoons lemon juice
- 1 tablespoon fresh parsley, chopped
- Salt and pepper to taste

For the Herbed Quinoa:

- 1 cup quinoa, rinsed
- 2 cups water or low-sodium chicken broth
- 2 tablespoons olive oil
- 2 cloves garlic, minced
- 2 tablespoons fresh herbs (such as parsley, basil, or dill), chopped
- Salt and pepper to taste

Instructions:

Prepare the Grilled Salmon:
- In a small bowl, whisk together the olive oil, minced garlic, lemon zest, lemon juice, chopped parsley, salt, and pepper.
- Place the salmon fillets in a shallow dish and pour the marinade over them, turning to coat evenly. Let the salmon marinate in the refrigerator for at least 30 minutes, up to 2 hours.

Preheat the Grill:
- Preheat your grill to medium-high heat. Make sure the grill grates are clean and lightly oiled to prevent sticking.

Grill the Salmon:
- Remove the salmon fillets from the marinade and shake off any excess.

- Place the salmon fillets on the preheated grill, skin-side down if using skin-on fillets.
- Grill the salmon for about 4-5 minutes per side, or until the fish flakes easily with a fork and is cooked to your desired level of doneness.

Prepare the Herbed Quinoa:

- In a medium saucepan, combine the rinsed quinoa and water or chicken broth. Bring to a boil over high heat.
- Once boiling, reduce the heat to low, cover, and simmer for about 15-20 minutes, or until the quinoa is cooked and all the liquid is absorbed.
- In a separate skillet, heat the olive oil over medium heat. Add the minced garlic and cook for 1-2 minutes, until fragrant.
- Stir the cooked quinoa into the skillet with the garlic. Add the chopped fresh herbs and season with salt and pepper to taste. Stir to combine.

Serve:

- Serve the grilled salmon hot with the herbed quinoa on the side.
- Garnish with additional fresh herbs and lemon wedges if desired.

Enjoy your Grilled Salmon with Herbed Quinoa! This dish is light, flavorful, and packed with protein and nutrients. It's perfect for a healthy and satisfying meal.

Roasted Garlic and Rosemary Pork Tenderloin

Ingredients:

- 2 pork tenderloins (about 1 lb each)
- 4 cloves garlic, minced
- 2 tablespoons fresh rosemary leaves, chopped
- 2 tablespoons olive oil
- 1 tablespoon balsamic vinegar
- 1 teaspoon honey
- Salt and pepper to taste

Instructions:

Preheat the Oven: Preheat your oven to 400°F (200°C).

Prepare the Marinade: In a small bowl, mix together the minced garlic, chopped rosemary leaves, olive oil, balsamic vinegar, honey, salt, and pepper.

Marinate the Pork: Place the pork tenderloins in a shallow dish or resealable plastic bag. Pour the marinade over the pork, making sure to coat them evenly. Let the pork marinate in the refrigerator for at least 30 minutes, or up to 4 hours for best flavor.

Roast the Pork: Remove the pork tenderloins from the marinade and place them on a roasting pan or baking sheet lined with parchment paper. Discard any remaining marinade.

Roast in the Oven: Roast the pork tenderloins in the preheated oven for 20-25 minutes, or until a meat thermometer inserted into the thickest part registers 145°F (63°C) for medium-rare, or 160°F (71°C) for medium. Cooking time may vary depending on the thickness of the tenderloins.

Rest and Serve: Once cooked, remove the pork tenderloins from the oven and let them rest for 5-10 minutes before slicing. This allows the juices to redistribute and ensures a juicy and tender result.

Slice and Serve: Slice the pork tenderloins into medallions and serve hot, garnished with additional fresh rosemary leaves if desired.

Optional Pan Sauce: If desired, you can make a simple pan sauce by deglazing the roasting pan with a splash of chicken broth or white wine and reducing it slightly. Season with salt and pepper to taste and drizzle over the sliced pork before serving.

Enjoy your Roasted Garlic and Rosemary Pork Tenderloin! It's a delicious and flavorful dish that's perfect for a special dinner or any day of the week.

Lemon Garlic Shrimp Stir-Fry

Ingredients:

- 1 lb (450g) large shrimp, peeled and deveined
- 2 tablespoons olive oil
- 4 cloves garlic, minced
- 1 tablespoon ginger, minced
- Zest of 1 lemon
- Juice of 1 lemon
- 1 tablespoon soy sauce
- 2 tablespoons honey or brown sugar
- 1 bell pepper, thinly sliced
- 1 cup snow peas, trimmed
- 1 carrot, julienned
- Salt and pepper to taste
- Cooked rice or noodles for serving
- Fresh cilantro or parsley for garnish (optional)

Instructions:

Prepare the Shrimp: Pat the shrimp dry with paper towels and season with salt and pepper.
Make the Sauce: In a small bowl, whisk together the minced garlic, minced ginger, lemon zest, lemon juice, soy sauce, and honey or brown sugar. Set aside.
Stir-Fry the Vegetables: Heat 1 tablespoon of olive oil in a large skillet or wok over medium-high heat. Add the sliced bell pepper, snow peas, and julienned carrot to the skillet. Stir-fry for 2-3 minutes, or until the vegetables are crisp-tender. Remove the vegetables from the skillet and set aside.
Cook the Shrimp: In the same skillet, add the remaining tablespoon of olive oil. Add the seasoned shrimp to the skillet and cook for 2-3 minutes, stirring occasionally, until the shrimp are pink and opaque.
Combine Everything: Return the cooked vegetables to the skillet with the shrimp. Pour the prepared sauce over the shrimp and vegetables, stirring to coat everything evenly. Cook for an additional 1-2 minutes, or until the sauce has thickened slightly and the shrimp are heated through.
Serve: Serve the lemon garlic shrimp stir-fry hot over cooked rice or noodles. Garnish with fresh cilantro or parsley, if desired.

Enjoy: Enjoy your delicious and flavorful Lemon Garlic Shrimp Stir-Fry!

This dish is quick and easy to make, packed with vibrant flavors, and perfect for a healthy and satisfying meal. Feel free to customize the vegetables or add additional ingredients to suit your taste preferences.

Herb-Roasted Turkey Breast

Ingredients:

- 1 bone-in turkey breast (about 4-5 pounds)
- 2 tablespoons olive oil
- 2 cloves garlic, minced
- 2 teaspoons dried thyme
- 2 teaspoons dried rosemary
- 2 teaspoons dried sage
- 1 teaspoon dried oregano
- Salt and pepper to taste
- 1 lemon, halved
- 1 onion, quartered
- 2 carrots, cut into chunks
- 2 stalks celery, cut into chunks
- 1 cup chicken or turkey broth

Instructions:

Preheat the Oven: Preheat your oven to 375°F (190°C).
Prepare the Turkey Breast: Rinse the turkey breast under cold water and pat it dry with paper towels. Place it on a roasting rack set inside a roasting pan.
Make the Herb Rub: In a small bowl, mix together the olive oil, minced garlic, dried thyme, dried rosemary, dried sage, dried oregano, salt, and pepper to form a paste.
Season the Turkey: Rub the herb paste all over the surface of the turkey breast, making sure to coat it evenly.
Add Aromatics: Squeeze the lemon halves over the turkey breast, then place them inside the cavity along with the onion quarters, carrots, and celery.
Roast the Turkey: Pour the chicken or turkey broth into the bottom of the roasting pan. Place the pan in the preheated oven and roast the turkey breast for about 1 ½ to 2 hours, or until the internal temperature reaches 165°F (75°C) when measured with a meat thermometer inserted into the thickest part of the breast.
Baste and Finish Cooking: Baste the turkey breast with the pan juices every 30 minutes while it cooks. If the skin starts to brown too quickly, tent it loosely with aluminum foil to prevent over-browning.

Rest and Serve: Once the turkey breast is cooked through, remove it from the oven and let it rest for at least 10-15 minutes before slicing. This allows the juices to redistribute and ensures a juicy and tender result.

Slice and Serve: Carve the herb-roasted turkey breast into slices and serve hot with your favorite side dishes.

Enjoy: Enjoy your delicious and aromatic Herb-Roasted Turkey Breast!

This recipe produces a flavorful and moist turkey breast with the perfect balance of herbs and spices. It's a great option for smaller gatherings or when you're craving turkey outside of the holiday season.

Baked Cod with Mediterranean Vegetables

Ingredients:

- 4 cod fillets
- 2 bell peppers (red and yellow), sliced
- 1 red onion, sliced
- 2 cloves garlic, minced
- 1 zucchini, sliced
- 1 cup cherry tomatoes
- 1/4 cup Kalamata olives, pitted
- 2 tablespoons olive oil
- 1 teaspoon dried oregano
- 1 teaspoon dried thyme
- Salt and pepper to taste
- Lemon wedges for serving
- Fresh parsley, chopped (for garnish)

Instructions:

Preheat your oven to 400°F (200°C). Lightly grease a baking dish with olive oil or cooking spray.

In a large bowl, combine the sliced bell peppers, red onion, minced garlic, zucchini, cherry tomatoes, and Kalamata olives. Drizzle with olive oil and sprinkle with dried oregano, dried thyme, salt, and pepper. Toss everything together until the vegetables are evenly coated.

Spread the vegetable mixture evenly in the prepared baking dish.

Season the cod fillets with salt and pepper on both sides. Place the cod fillets on top of the vegetables in the baking dish.

Drizzle a little more olive oil over the cod fillets and vegetables.

Bake in the preheated oven for about 15-20 minutes, or until the cod is cooked through and flakes easily with a fork, and the vegetables are tender.

Once done, remove from the oven and garnish with fresh parsley. Serve hot with lemon wedges on the side.

Enjoy your baked cod with Mediterranean vegetables! It pairs well with couscous, rice, or crusty bread.

Quinoa and Black Bean Stuffed Peppers

Ingredients:

- 4 large bell peppers, any color
- 1 cup quinoa, rinsed
- 1 can (15 ounces) black beans, drained and rinsed
- 1 cup corn kernels (fresh, frozen, or canned)
- 1 small onion, finely chopped
- 2 cloves garlic, minced
- 1 teaspoon ground cumin
- 1 teaspoon chili powder
- 1/2 teaspoon paprika
- Salt and pepper to taste
- 1 cup shredded cheese (cheddar, Monterey Jack, or a blend)
- Fresh cilantro, chopped, for garnish (optional)
- Avocado slices, for serving (optional)
- Sour cream or Greek yogurt, for serving (optional)

Instructions:

Preheat your oven to 375°F (190°C). Lightly grease a baking dish large enough to hold the stuffed peppers.

Cut the tops off the bell peppers and remove the seeds and membranes. Rinse the peppers under cold water.

In a medium saucepan, combine the quinoa with 2 cups of water. Bring to a boil, then reduce the heat to low, cover, and simmer for about 15 minutes, or until the quinoa is cooked and the water is absorbed.

In a large skillet, heat a little olive oil over medium heat. Add the chopped onion and cook until softened, about 3-4 minutes. Add the minced garlic and cook for another minute, until fragrant.

Add the cooked quinoa, black beans, corn, ground cumin, chili powder, paprika, salt, and pepper to the skillet. Stir everything together and cook for a few minutes until heated through.

Remove the skillet from the heat and stir in half of the shredded cheese.

Stuff the bell peppers with the quinoa and black bean mixture, packing it down gently. Place the stuffed peppers upright in the prepared baking dish.

Sprinkle the remaining shredded cheese over the tops of the stuffed peppers.

Cover the baking dish with foil and bake in the preheated oven for about 25-30 minutes, or until the peppers are tender.
Remove the foil and bake for an additional 5-10 minutes, or until the cheese is melted and bubbly.
Once done, remove from the oven and let the stuffed peppers cool for a few minutes before serving.
Garnish with chopped cilantro, if desired, and serve with avocado slices and sour cream or Greek yogurt on the side.

Enjoy your delicious quinoa and black bean stuffed peppers! They make a satisfying and wholesome meal.

Turkey Meatball and Vegetable Soup

Ingredients:

For the turkey meatballs:

- 1 pound ground turkey
- 1/2 cup breadcrumbs
- 1/4 cup grated Parmesan cheese
- 1 egg, lightly beaten
- 2 cloves garlic, minced
- 2 tablespoons fresh parsley, chopped
- Salt and pepper to taste

For the soup:

- 1 tablespoon olive oil
- 1 onion, chopped
- 2 carrots, diced
- 2 celery stalks, diced
- 2 cloves garlic, minced
- 6 cups chicken or vegetable broth
- 1 can (14.5 ounces) diced tomatoes
- 1 teaspoon dried oregano
- 1 teaspoon dried thyme
- Salt and pepper to taste
- 2 cups baby spinach or kale, chopped
- Fresh parsley, chopped, for garnish (optional)
- Grated Parmesan cheese, for serving (optional)

Instructions:

In a large bowl, combine the ground turkey, breadcrumbs, grated Parmesan cheese, egg, minced garlic, chopped parsley, salt, and pepper. Mix until well combined.

Shape the turkey mixture into small meatballs, about 1 inch in diameter. You should get around 20-24 meatballs depending on the size.

In a large pot or Dutch oven, heat the olive oil over medium heat. Add the chopped onion, carrots, and celery. Cook, stirring occasionally, until the vegetables are softened, about 5-6 minutes.

Add the minced garlic to the pot and cook for another minute, until fragrant.

Pour in the chicken or vegetable broth and diced tomatoes with their juices. Stir in the dried oregano, dried thyme, salt, and pepper. Bring the soup to a simmer.

Carefully add the turkey meatballs to the simmering soup. Let the meatballs cook for about 10-12 minutes, or until cooked through.

Once the meatballs are cooked, add the chopped baby spinach or kale to the soup. Cook for an additional 2-3 minutes, until the greens are wilted.

Taste the soup and adjust the seasoning with salt and pepper if needed.

Ladle the turkey meatball and vegetable soup into bowls. Garnish with chopped parsley and grated Parmesan cheese if desired.

Serve hot and enjoy your delicious and nutritious soup!

This soup is great served with crusty bread or a side salad for a complete meal.

Grilled Chicken Caesar Salad

Ingredients:

For the grilled chicken:

- 2 boneless, skinless chicken breasts
- Salt and pepper to taste
- 2 tablespoons olive oil
- 2 cloves garlic, minced
- 1 teaspoon dried oregano
- 1 teaspoon dried thyme
- Juice of 1 lemon

For the Caesar dressing:

- 1/2 cup mayonnaise
- 2 tablespoons grated Parmesan cheese
- 2 tablespoons freshly squeezed lemon juice
- 1 clove garlic, minced
- 1 teaspoon Dijon mustard
- Salt and pepper to taste

For the salad:

- 1 large head of romaine lettuce, washed and chopped
- 1/2 cup croutons
- 1/4 cup grated Parmesan cheese
- Extra Parmesan cheese for garnish (optional)
- Lemon wedges for serving (optional)

Instructions:

Preheat your grill to medium-high heat.
Season the chicken breasts with salt and pepper on both sides.
In a small bowl, whisk together the olive oil, minced garlic, dried oregano, dried thyme, and lemon juice. Brush the mixture over the chicken breasts, coating them evenly.
Grill the chicken breasts for about 6-8 minutes per side, or until cooked through and no longer pink in the center. Cooking time may vary depending on the

thickness of the chicken breasts. Remove from the grill and let them rest for a few minutes before slicing.

While the chicken is grilling, prepare the Caesar dressing. In a bowl, combine the mayonnaise, grated Parmesan cheese, lemon juice, minced garlic, Dijon mustard, salt, and pepper. Whisk until smooth and well combined. Adjust the seasoning to taste.

In a large salad bowl, toss the chopped romaine lettuce with the Caesar dressing until evenly coated.

Divide the dressed lettuce among serving plates. Top each plate with sliced grilled chicken.

Sprinkle croutons and grated Parmesan cheese over the salads.

If desired, garnish with extra Parmesan cheese and serve with lemon wedges on the side.

Serve immediately and enjoy your delicious grilled chicken Caesar salad!

This salad makes for a satisfying and flavorful meal, perfect for lunch or dinner. Feel free to customize it by adding cherry tomatoes, avocado slices, or crispy bacon if desired.

Broiled Tilapia with Lemon-Dill Sauce

Ingredients:

For the tilapia:

- 4 tilapia fillets
- 2 tablespoons olive oil
- Salt and pepper to taste
- 1 lemon, thinly sliced (for garnish)

For the lemon-dill sauce:

- 1/2 cup mayonnaise
- 2 tablespoons freshly squeezed lemon juice
- 1 tablespoon chopped fresh dill (or 1 teaspoon dried dill)
- 1 clove garlic, minced
- Salt and pepper to taste

Instructions:

Preheat your broiler to high and place the oven rack about 6 inches below the heat source. Line a baking sheet with aluminum foil and lightly grease it with olive oil or cooking spray.

Pat the tilapia fillets dry with paper towels. Brush both sides of the fillets with olive oil and season them with salt and pepper.

Place the seasoned tilapia fillets on the prepared baking sheet in a single layer. Broil the tilapia for 4-6 minutes on each side, or until the fish is opaque and flakes easily with a fork. Cooking time may vary depending on the thickness of the fillets.

While the tilapia is broiling, prepare the lemon-dill sauce. In a small bowl, combine the mayonnaise, lemon juice, chopped fresh dill, minced garlic, salt, and pepper. Stir until well combined. Taste and adjust the seasoning if needed.

Once the tilapia is cooked through, remove it from the oven and transfer the fillets to serving plates.

Drizzle the lemon-dill sauce over the broiled tilapia fillets.

Garnish with lemon slices and additional chopped fresh dill, if desired.

Serve immediately, and enjoy your delicious broiled tilapia with lemon-dill sauce!

This dish pairs well with steamed vegetables, rice, or roasted potatoes. It's perfect for a light and healthy dinner option.

Roasted Vegetable and Chickpea Salad

Ingredients:

For the roasted vegetables:

- 2 cups cauliflower florets
- 2 cups cherry tomatoes
- 1 red bell pepper, sliced
- 1 yellow bell pepper, sliced
- 1 small red onion, sliced
- 2 tablespoons olive oil
- 1 teaspoon dried oregano
- 1 teaspoon dried thyme
- Salt and pepper to taste

For the chickpeas:

- 1 can (15 ounces) chickpeas, drained and rinsed
- 1 tablespoon olive oil
- 1 teaspoon ground cumin
- 1/2 teaspoon smoked paprika
- Salt and pepper to taste

For the salad:

- 4 cups mixed salad greens (such as spinach, arugula, or lettuce)
- 1/4 cup crumbled feta cheese (optional)
- 1/4 cup chopped fresh parsley or cilantro (for garnish)

For the dressing:

- 3 tablespoons olive oil
- 2 tablespoons balsamic vinegar
- 1 tablespoon honey or maple syrup
- 1 teaspoon Dijon mustard
- Salt and pepper to taste

Instructions:

Preheat your oven to 400°F (200°C). Line a baking sheet with parchment paper or aluminum foil for easy cleanup.

In a large bowl, toss together the cauliflower florets, cherry tomatoes, sliced bell peppers, and red onion with olive oil, dried oregano, dried thyme, salt, and pepper until evenly coated.

Spread the seasoned vegetables in a single layer on the prepared baking sheet. Roast in the preheated oven for about 25-30 minutes, or until the vegetables are tender and lightly browned, stirring halfway through.

While the vegetables are roasting, prepare the chickpeas. In a separate bowl, toss the drained and rinsed chickpeas with olive oil, ground cumin, smoked paprika, salt, and pepper until coated.

Spread the seasoned chickpeas on a separate baking sheet or the same one if there's space. Roast in the oven alongside the vegetables for about 20-25 minutes, or until crispy, shaking the pan occasionally.

In a small bowl, whisk together the ingredients for the dressing: olive oil, balsamic vinegar, honey or maple syrup, Dijon mustard, salt, and pepper.

Once the vegetables and chickpeas are roasted, remove them from the oven and let them cool slightly.

In a large salad bowl, combine the mixed salad greens with the roasted vegetables and chickpeas.

Drizzle the dressing over the salad and toss gently to combine.

Sprinkle crumbled feta cheese over the salad if desired.

Garnish with chopped fresh parsley or cilantro.

Serve the roasted vegetable and chickpea salad immediately as a main course or a side dish.

Enjoy your delicious and nutritious salad! It's packed with flavor and makes for a satisfying meal.

Low-Sodium Beef and Vegetable Stir-Fry

Ingredients:

For the stir-fry sauce:

- 1/4 cup low-sodium soy sauce
- 2 tablespoons water
- 1 tablespoon rice vinegar
- 1 tablespoon honey or maple syrup
- 1 teaspoon cornstarch

For the stir-fry:

- 1 pound flank steak, thinly sliced against the grain
- 2 tablespoons vegetable oil, divided
- 3 cloves garlic, minced
- 1 tablespoon grated ginger
- 1 onion, thinly sliced
- 2 bell peppers (any color), thinly sliced
- 2 cups broccoli florets
- 1 cup sliced mushrooms
- 1 cup snow peas, trimmed
- Cooked brown rice or quinoa, for serving
- Sesame seeds and chopped green onions, for garnish (optional)

Instructions:

In a small bowl, whisk together the low-sodium soy sauce, water, rice vinegar, honey or maple syrup, and cornstarch to make the stir-fry sauce. Set aside.
Heat 1 tablespoon of vegetable oil in a large skillet or wok over medium-high heat.
Add the thinly sliced flank steak to the skillet in a single layer. Cook for 2-3 minutes without stirring to allow the steak to sear and develop a brown crust. Flip the steak slices and cook for an additional 1-2 minutes until browned. Remove the steak from the skillet and set aside.
In the same skillet, add the remaining tablespoon of vegetable oil.

Add the minced garlic and grated ginger to the skillet. Stir-fry for about 30 seconds until fragrant.

Add the thinly sliced onion, bell peppers, broccoli florets, sliced mushrooms, and snow peas to the skillet. Stir-fry for 4-5 minutes, or until the vegetables are tender-crisp.

Return the cooked flank steak to the skillet with the vegetables.

Pour the stir-fry sauce over the beef and vegetables in the skillet. Cook, stirring constantly, for 1-2 minutes until the sauce thickens and coats the beef and vegetables.

Remove the skillet from the heat.

Serve the low-sodium beef and vegetable stir-fry hot over cooked brown rice or quinoa.

Garnish with sesame seeds and chopped green onions if desired.

Enjoy your flavorful and nutritious low-sodium beef and vegetable stir-fry! Adjust the vegetables according to your preferences and feel free to add other low-sodium seasonings or herbs for extra flavor.

Herbed Roast Beef with Red Wine Reduction

Ingredients:

For the roast beef:

- 1 (3-4 pound) beef sirloin roast or beef tenderloin
- 2 tablespoons olive oil
- 3 cloves garlic, minced
- 1 tablespoon chopped fresh rosemary
- 1 tablespoon chopped fresh thyme
- 1 tablespoon chopped fresh parsley
- Salt and pepper to taste

For the red wine reduction:

- 1 cup red wine (such as Cabernet Sauvignon or Merlot)
- 1 cup beef broth
- 2 tablespoons unsalted butter
- 1 shallot, finely chopped
- 2 cloves garlic, minced
- Salt and pepper to taste

Instructions:

Preheat your oven to 375°F (190°C).
In a small bowl, combine the olive oil, minced garlic, chopped fresh rosemary, thyme, parsley, salt, and pepper to make the herb rub.
Pat the beef roast dry with paper towels. Rub the herb mixture all over the surface of the roast, ensuring it's evenly coated.
Place the seasoned roast on a rack set in a roasting pan, fat side up.
Roast the beef in the preheated oven for about 20-25 minutes per pound for medium-rare, or until the internal temperature reaches 135°F (57°C) for medium-rare or 145°F (63°C) for medium, using a meat thermometer inserted into the thickest part of the roast.

Once the roast reaches the desired doneness, remove it from the oven and transfer it to a cutting board. Cover loosely with aluminum foil and let it rest for about 15 minutes before slicing.

While the roast is resting, make the red wine reduction. In a saucepan, melt the butter over medium heat.

Add the chopped shallot and minced garlic to the saucepan. Cook, stirring occasionally, until softened and fragrant, about 2-3 minutes.

Pour in the red wine and beef broth. Bring the mixture to a simmer and cook until the liquid is reduced by half, stirring occasionally, about 10-15 minutes.

Season the red wine reduction with salt and pepper to taste.

Once the roast beef has rested, slice it thinly against the grain.

Serve the sliced roast beef with the red wine reduction drizzled over the top. Garnish with fresh herbs if desired.

Enjoy your herbed roast beef with red wine reduction! This dish pairs well with roasted vegetables, mashed potatoes, or a green salad for a complete meal.

Lemon Herb Baked Chicken Thighs

Ingredients:

- 6-8 chicken thighs, bone-in and skin-on
- 2 tablespoons olive oil
- Zest of 1 lemon
- Juice of 1 lemon
- 3 cloves garlic, minced
- 1 tablespoon chopped fresh parsley
- 1 tablespoon chopped fresh thyme
- 1 teaspoon chopped fresh rosemary
- Salt and pepper to taste
- Lemon slices for garnish (optional)
- Fresh parsley for garnish (optional)

Instructions:

Preheat your oven to 400°F (200°C). Line a baking dish with parchment paper or aluminum foil for easy cleanup.

In a small bowl, combine the olive oil, lemon zest, lemon juice, minced garlic, chopped fresh parsley, thyme, rosemary, salt, and pepper. Mix well to make the marinade.

Place the chicken thighs in a large bowl or resealable plastic bag. Pour the marinade over the chicken thighs, ensuring they are evenly coated. Allow the chicken to marinate for at least 30 minutes in the refrigerator, or overnight for best flavor.

Arrange the marinated chicken thighs in a single layer in the prepared baking dish, skin-side up.

Drizzle any remaining marinade over the chicken thighs.

Bake in the preheated oven for 35-40 minutes, or until the chicken is cooked through and the skin is golden brown and crispy. The internal temperature should reach 165°F (74°C) when measured with a meat thermometer inserted into the thickest part of the thigh, avoiding the bone.

Once done, remove the chicken thighs from the oven and let them rest for a few minutes before serving.

Garnish with lemon slices and fresh parsley, if desired.

Serve the lemon herb baked chicken thighs hot with your favorite side dishes, such as roasted vegetables, mashed potatoes, or a salad.

Enjoy your flavorful and juicy lemon herb baked chicken thighs! This dish is sure to become a family favorite.

Eggplant and Tomato Gratin

Ingredients:

- 2 medium eggplants, sliced into rounds
- 4 ripe tomatoes, sliced
- 2 cloves garlic, minced
- 1/4 cup chopped fresh basil leaves
- 1/4 cup chopped fresh parsley
- 1/2 cup grated Parmesan cheese
- 1/4 cup breadcrumbs
- Salt and pepper to taste
- Olive oil for drizzling

Instructions:

Preheat your oven to 375°F (190°C). Lightly grease a baking dish with olive oil or cooking spray.
Arrange the eggplant slices in a single layer on a baking sheet. Drizzle them with olive oil and season with salt and pepper.
Roast the eggplant slices in the preheated oven for about 15-20 minutes, or until they are tender and lightly browned. Remove from the oven and set aside.
In a small bowl, combine the minced garlic, chopped basil, chopped parsley, grated Parmesan cheese, and breadcrumbs. Mix well to combine.
Arrange a layer of roasted eggplant slices in the bottom of the prepared baking dish.
Top the eggplant slices with a layer of sliced tomatoes.
Sprinkle the garlic and herb mixture evenly over the tomatoes.
Repeat the layers until all the eggplant and tomatoes are used, finishing with a layer of the garlic and herb mixture on top.
Drizzle a little more olive oil over the top of the gratin.
Cover the baking dish with aluminum foil and bake in the preheated oven for about 20-25 minutes.
Remove the foil and bake for an additional 10-15 minutes, or until the gratin is golden brown and bubbling.
Once done, remove from the oven and let it cool for a few minutes before serving.
Serve the eggplant and tomato gratin warm as a side dish or as a main course with a salad and crusty bread.

Enjoy your delicious and flavorful eggplant and tomato gratin! It's a perfect dish for showcasing the flavors of fresh summer produce.

Grilled Portobello Mushrooms with Balsamic Glaze

Ingredients:

For the grilled portobello mushrooms:

- 4 large portobello mushrooms, stems removed
- 2 tablespoons olive oil
- 2 cloves garlic, minced
- Salt and pepper to taste

For the balsamic glaze:

- 1/2 cup balsamic vinegar
- 2 tablespoons honey or maple syrup
- 1 clove garlic, minced
- Salt and pepper to taste

Instructions:

Preheat your grill to medium-high heat.
In a small bowl, whisk together the olive oil, minced garlic, salt, and pepper.
Brush both sides of the portobello mushrooms with the olive oil mixture.
Place the mushrooms on the preheated grill, gill side down. Grill for about 4-5 minutes on each side, or until the mushrooms are tender and grill marks appear.
While the mushrooms are grilling, prepare the balsamic glaze. In a small saucepan, combine the balsamic vinegar, honey or maple syrup, minced garlic, salt, and pepper.
Bring the mixture to a simmer over medium heat. Cook, stirring occasionally, until the glaze has thickened and reduced by about half, about 10-15 minutes. Be careful not to let it burn.
Once the mushrooms are grilled to your liking, remove them from the grill and place them on a serving platter.
Drizzle the balsamic glaze over the grilled portobello mushrooms.
Serve the mushrooms hot, garnished with fresh herbs if desired.

Enjoy your delicious grilled portobello mushrooms with balsamic glaze! They make a flavorful and elegant dish that's perfect for any occasion. You can serve them as a main course with a side salad or as a side dish alongside grilled vegetables or roasted potatoes.

Low-Sodium Minestrone Soup

Ingredients:

- 2 tablespoons olive oil
- 1 onion, diced
- 2 carrots, diced
- 2 celery stalks, diced
- 3 cloves garlic, minced
- 1 zucchini, diced
- 1 yellow squash, diced
- 1 cup green beans, chopped
- 1 can (14.5 ounces) diced tomatoes, with their juices
- 6 cups low-sodium vegetable broth or chicken broth
- 1 teaspoon dried oregano
- 1 teaspoon dried basil
- 1/2 teaspoon dried thyme
- 1 bay leaf
- 1 cup small pasta (such as ditalini or small shells)
- 1 can (15 ounces) kidney beans, drained and rinsed
- 1 can (15 ounces) cannellini beans, drained and rinsed
- Salt-free Italian seasoning blend, to taste
- Freshly ground black pepper, to taste
- Fresh parsley, chopped, for garnish
- Grated Parmesan cheese (optional), for serving

Instructions:

Heat the olive oil in a large pot over medium heat. Add the diced onion, carrots, and celery. Cook, stirring occasionally, until the vegetables are softened, about 5-7 minutes.

Add the minced garlic to the pot and cook for another minute until fragrant.

Stir in the diced zucchini, yellow squash, and chopped green beans. Cook for a few more minutes until the vegetables start to soften.

Add the diced tomatoes (with their juices) to the pot, along with the low-sodium vegetable broth or chicken broth.

Stir in the dried oregano, dried basil, dried thyme, and bay leaf. Bring the soup to a simmer.

Once the soup is simmering, add the small pasta to the pot. Cook according to the package instructions until the pasta is al dente.
Stir in the drained and rinsed kidney beans and cannellini beans.
Season the soup with salt-free Italian seasoning blend and freshly ground black pepper, to taste. Adjust the seasoning as needed.
Simmer the soup for a few more minutes to allow the flavors to meld together. Once done, remove the bay leaf from the soup.
Ladle the low-sodium minestrone soup into bowls. Garnish with chopped fresh parsley and grated Parmesan cheese, if desired.
Serve hot and enjoy your flavorful and nutritious low-sodium minestrone soup!

This soup is hearty and satisfying, packed with a variety of vegetables and beans. It's perfect for a comforting meal, especially on a chilly day.

Baked Lemon Pepper Chicken Breasts

Ingredients:

- 4 boneless, skinless chicken breasts
- 2 tablespoons olive oil
- 2 tablespoons lemon juice
- 2 teaspoons lemon zest
- 2 teaspoons freshly ground black pepper
- 1 teaspoon garlic powder
- 1 teaspoon onion powder
- 1 teaspoon dried thyme
- 1 teaspoon dried parsley
- Salt to taste
- Lemon slices for garnish (optional)
- Fresh parsley for garnish (optional)

Instructions:

Preheat your oven to 400°F (200°C). Lightly grease a baking dish with olive oil or cooking spray.

In a small bowl, whisk together the olive oil, lemon juice, lemon zest, black pepper, garlic powder, onion powder, dried thyme, dried parsley, and salt to taste.

Place the chicken breasts in the prepared baking dish in a single layer.

Pour the lemon pepper marinade over the chicken breasts, making sure they are evenly coated on both sides. You can use a brush or your hands to spread the marinade.

If time allows, let the chicken marinate in the refrigerator for about 30 minutes to 1 hour to allow the flavors to penetrate the meat. If you're in a hurry, you can bake it immediately.

Bake the chicken breasts in the preheated oven for about 20-25 minutes, or until they are cooked through and reach an internal temperature of 165°F (74°C) when tested with a meat thermometer inserted into the thickest part of the breast.

If desired, you can broil the chicken for an additional 2-3 minutes at the end to brown the tops and add some extra color and flavor.

Once done, remove the chicken breasts from the oven and let them rest for a few minutes before serving.

Garnish the baked lemon pepper chicken breasts with lemon slices and fresh parsley, if desired.
Serve hot and enjoy your flavorful and juicy baked lemon pepper chicken breasts!

This dish pairs well with steamed vegetables, rice, or roasted potatoes. It's a versatile and delicious recipe that's sure to become a favorite in your meal rotation.

Spaghetti Squash with Marinara Sauce

Ingredients:

- 1 spaghetti squash
- 2 tablespoons olive oil
- Salt and pepper to taste
- 2 cups marinara sauce (store-bought or homemade)
- Grated Parmesan cheese for serving (optional)
- Fresh basil leaves for garnish (optional)

Instructions:

Preheat your oven to 400°F (200°C).
Cut the spaghetti squash in half lengthwise and scoop out the seeds and stringy pulp from the center using a spoon.
Brush the cut sides of the spaghetti squash halves with olive oil and sprinkle with salt and pepper.
Place the spaghetti squash halves, cut side down, on a baking sheet lined with parchment paper or aluminum foil.
Bake the spaghetti squash in the preheated oven for about 35-45 minutes, or until the flesh is tender and easily pierced with a fork.
Once the spaghetti squash is cooked, remove it from the oven and let it cool for a few minutes.
Use a fork to scrape the flesh of the spaghetti squash into strands. Transfer the spaghetti squash strands to a serving dish.
Heat the marinara sauce in a saucepan over medium heat until warmed through.
Pour the marinara sauce over the spaghetti squash strands and toss gently to coat.
Serve the spaghetti squash with marinara sauce hot, garnished with grated Parmesan cheese and fresh basil leaves if desired.
Enjoy your delicious and healthy spaghetti squash with marinara sauce as a light and satisfying meal!

You can customize this dish by adding cooked meatballs, sautéed vegetables, or other toppings of your choice. It's a great option for those looking to reduce their carb intake or incorporate more vegetables into their diet.

Turkey and Vegetable Stir-Fry

Ingredients:

- 1 lb (450g) turkey breast or turkey tenderloins, thinly sliced
- 2 tablespoons soy sauce
- 1 tablespoon oyster sauce
- 1 tablespoon hoisin sauce
- 1 tablespoon cornstarch
- 2 tablespoons vegetable oil
- 2 cloves garlic, minced
- 1 tablespoon ginger, minced
- 1 onion, sliced
- 2 bell peppers (any color), thinly sliced
- 1 cup broccoli florets
- 1 cup sliced carrots
- 1 cup sliced mushrooms
- Salt and pepper to taste
- Cooked rice or noodles for serving
- Optional garnish: chopped green onions, sesame seeds

Instructions:

In a bowl, combine the soy sauce, oyster sauce, hoisin sauce, and cornstarch. Add the thinly sliced turkey to the bowl and toss to coat the turkey in the marinade. Let it marinate for about 15-20 minutes.

Heat 1 tablespoon of vegetable oil in a large skillet or wok over medium-high heat. Add the marinated turkey to the skillet and stir-fry for 3-4 minutes, or until the turkey is cooked through. Remove the turkey from the skillet and set it aside on a plate.

In the same skillet, add the remaining tablespoon of vegetable oil. Add the minced garlic and ginger, and cook for about 1 minute, until fragrant.

Add the sliced onion, bell peppers, broccoli florets, carrots, and mushrooms to the skillet. Stir-fry for 4-5 minutes, or until the vegetables are tender-crisp.

Return the cooked turkey to the skillet with the vegetables. Stir everything together and cook for an additional 1-2 minutes to heat through.

Season the stir-fry with salt and pepper to taste.

Serve the turkey and vegetable stir-fry hot over cooked rice or noodles.

Garnish with chopped green onions and sesame seeds if desired.

Enjoy your delicious and nutritious turkey and vegetable stir-fry! It's a versatile dish, so feel free to customize it with your favorite vegetables and adjust the seasonings to your taste.

Poached Salmon with Dill Sauce

Ingredients:

For the poached salmon:

- 4 salmon fillets, about 6 ounces each
- 4 cups water or vegetable broth
- 1 lemon, sliced
- 1 small onion, sliced
- 2 bay leaves
- Salt and pepper to taste

For the dill sauce:

- 1/2 cup mayonnaise
- 1/2 cup sour cream or Greek yogurt
- 2 tablespoons freshly squeezed lemon juice
- 2 tablespoons chopped fresh dill
- 1 tablespoon chopped fresh parsley
- 1 tablespoon Dijon mustard
- Salt and pepper to taste

Instructions:

In a large skillet or shallow pan, combine the water or vegetable broth, sliced lemon, sliced onion, and bay leaves. Bring the liquid to a simmer over medium heat.

Season the salmon fillets with salt and pepper on both sides.

Carefully add the seasoned salmon fillets to the simmering liquid, ensuring they are submerged.

Cover the skillet with a lid and poach the salmon for about 8-10 minutes, or until the salmon is cooked through and flakes easily with a fork. Cooking time may vary depending on the thickness of the fillets.

While the salmon is poaching, prepare the dill sauce. In a small bowl, combine the mayonnaise, sour cream or Greek yogurt, lemon juice, chopped dill, chopped parsley, Dijon mustard, salt, and pepper. Mix until well combined. Taste and adjust the seasoning if needed.

Once the salmon is cooked, carefully remove the fillets from the poaching liquid using a slotted spatula and transfer them to serving plates.

Spoon the dill sauce over the poached salmon fillets, or serve it on the side as a dipping sauce.

Garnish with additional chopped fresh dill and lemon slices if desired.

Serve the poached salmon with dill sauce immediately, accompanied by your favorite side dishes such as steamed vegetables, rice, or roasted potatoes.

Enjoy your delicious and tender poached salmon with creamy dill sauce! It's a light and flavorful dish that's sure to impress your guests.

Low-Sodium Chicken and Vegetable Curry

Ingredients:

- 1 lb (450g) boneless, skinless chicken breasts or thighs, cut into bite-sized pieces
- 2 tablespoons olive oil
- 1 onion, finely chopped
- 3 cloves garlic, minced
- 1 tablespoon grated ginger
- 2 tablespoons curry powder (adjust to taste)
- 1 teaspoon ground cumin
- 1 teaspoon ground coriander
- 1/2 teaspoon turmeric
- 1/4 teaspoon cayenne pepper (optional, for heat)
- 1 can (14 ounces) diced tomatoes, with their juices
- 1 cup low-sodium chicken broth
- 1 cup coconut milk (full-fat or light)
- 2 cups mixed vegetables (such as bell peppers, carrots, broccoli, peas)
- Salt to taste
- Fresh cilantro, chopped, for garnish
- Cooked rice or naan bread, for serving

Instructions:

Heat the olive oil in a large skillet or Dutch oven over medium heat. Add the chopped onion and cook until softened, about 5 minutes.

Add the minced garlic and grated ginger to the skillet and cook for another minute until fragrant.

Add the curry powder, ground cumin, ground coriander, turmeric, and cayenne pepper (if using) to the skillet. Stir well to coat the onions and spices.

Add the bite-sized chicken pieces to the skillet and cook until browned on all sides, about 5-7 minutes.

Pour in the diced tomatoes with their juices, low-sodium chicken broth, and coconut milk. Stir well to combine.

Bring the mixture to a simmer and let it cook for about 10 minutes to allow the flavors to meld together and the chicken to cook through.

Add the mixed vegetables to the skillet and simmer for an additional 5-10 minutes, or until the vegetables are tender.

Taste the curry and season with salt to taste. Adjust the seasoning as needed. Once done, remove the skillet from the heat and garnish the chicken and vegetable curry with chopped fresh cilantro.
Serve the low-sodium chicken and vegetable curry hot over cooked rice or with naan bread on the side.

Enjoy your flavorful and aromatic chicken and vegetable curry! This dish is packed with protein, vegetables, and spices, making it a satisfying and nutritious meal. Adjust the spice level and vegetables according to your taste preferences.

Roasted Brussels Sprouts with Garlic and Parmesan

Ingredients:

- 1 lb (450g) Brussels sprouts, trimmed and halved
- 2 tablespoons olive oil
- 4 cloves garlic, minced
- Salt and pepper to taste
- 1/4 cup grated Parmesan cheese
- Lemon wedges for serving (optional)

Instructions:

Preheat your oven to 400°F (200°C). Line a baking sheet with parchment paper or aluminum foil for easy cleanup.

In a large bowl, toss the halved Brussels sprouts with olive oil, minced garlic, salt, and pepper until evenly coated.

Spread the Brussels sprouts out in a single layer on the prepared baking sheet.

Roast the Brussels sprouts in the preheated oven for about 20-25 minutes, or until they are tender and caramelized, stirring halfway through the cooking time for even browning.

Once the Brussels sprouts are roasted to your liking, remove them from the oven and transfer them to a serving dish.

Sprinkle the grated Parmesan cheese over the roasted Brussels sprouts while they are still hot, allowing the cheese to melt slightly.

Serve the roasted Brussels sprouts with garlic and Parmesan immediately, garnished with lemon wedges if desired.

Enjoy your delicious and flavorful roasted Brussels sprouts as a side dish for any meal!

The combination of roasted Brussels sprouts with garlic and Parmesan cheese is sure to be a hit at your dinner table.

Herb-Crusted Pork Chops

Ingredients:

- 4 bone-in pork chops (about 3/4 inch thick)
- 2 tablespoons Dijon mustard
- 2 cloves garlic, minced
- 1 tablespoon chopped fresh rosemary
- 1 tablespoon chopped fresh thyme
- 1 tablespoon chopped fresh parsley
- 1/2 cup breadcrumbs (panko or regular)
- Salt and pepper to taste
- 2 tablespoons olive oil

Instructions:

Preheat your oven to 375°F (190°C). Line a baking sheet with parchment paper or aluminum foil for easy cleanup.

In a small bowl, mix together the Dijon mustard, minced garlic, chopped fresh rosemary, thyme, parsley, salt, and pepper.

Pat the pork chops dry with paper towels and season them lightly with salt and pepper on both sides.

Spread a thin layer of the Dijon mustard mixture evenly over each pork chop.

In another shallow dish, spread out the breadcrumbs.

Press each pork chop into the breadcrumbs, coating both sides evenly and pressing down gently to adhere.

Heat the olive oil in a large skillet over medium-high heat.

Once the oil is hot, add the pork chops to the skillet and cook for about 2-3 minutes on each side, or until golden brown.

Transfer the browned pork chops to the prepared baking sheet.

Bake the pork chops in the preheated oven for about 10-12 minutes, or until they reach an internal temperature of 145°F (63°C) when tested with a meat thermometer inserted into the thickest part of the chop.

Once done, remove the pork chops from the oven and let them rest for a few minutes before serving.

Serve the herb-crusted pork chops hot, garnished with additional fresh herbs if desired.

Enjoy your delicious and flavorful herb-crusted pork chops! They're perfect for a quick and satisfying meal any day of the week.

Lemon Garlic Roasted Chicken Drumsticks

Ingredients:

- 8 chicken drumsticks
- 4 cloves garlic, minced
- Zest of 1 lemon
- Juice of 1 lemon
- 2 tablespoons olive oil
- 1 teaspoon dried oregano
- 1 teaspoon dried thyme
- 1 teaspoon paprika
- Salt and pepper to taste
- Lemon slices for garnish (optional)
- Fresh parsley for garnish (optional)

Instructions:

Preheat your oven to 425°F (220°C). Line a baking sheet with parchment paper or aluminum foil for easy cleanup.

In a small bowl, combine the minced garlic, lemon zest, lemon juice, olive oil, dried oregano, dried thyme, paprika, salt, and pepper to make the marinade.

Pat the chicken drumsticks dry with paper towels and place them in a large bowl. Pour the marinade over the chicken drumsticks, making sure they are evenly coated. Use your hands to massage the marinade into the drumsticks.

Arrange the marinated chicken drumsticks on the prepared baking sheet in a single layer.

Roast the chicken drumsticks in the preheated oven for about 35-40 minutes, or until the chicken is golden brown and cooked through, with an internal temperature of 165°F (74°C) when tested with a meat thermometer inserted into the thickest part of the drumstick.

Once done, remove the chicken drumsticks from the oven and let them rest for a few minutes before serving.

Garnish the lemon garlic roasted chicken drumsticks with lemon slices and fresh parsley, if desired.

Serve hot and enjoy your flavorful and juicy chicken drumsticks!

These lemon garlic roasted chicken drumsticks are delicious served with roasted vegetables, mashed potatoes, or a green salad. They're sure to be a hit at the dinner table!

Grilled Vegetable and Quinoa Salad

Ingredients:

For the grilled vegetables:

- 2 bell peppers (any color), seeded and quartered
- 1 zucchini, sliced lengthwise
- 1 yellow squash, sliced lengthwise
- 1 red onion, sliced into thick rounds
- 1 tablespoon olive oil
- Salt and pepper to taste

For the quinoa:

- 1 cup quinoa, rinsed
- 2 cups water or vegetable broth
- Salt to taste

For the salad dressing:

- 1/4 cup olive oil
- 2 tablespoons balsamic vinegar
- 1 tablespoon Dijon mustard
- 1 clove garlic, minced
- Salt and pepper to taste

Additional salad ingredients:

- 1 cup cherry tomatoes, halved
- 1/4 cup chopped fresh basil leaves
- 1/4 cup crumbled feta cheese (optional)
- Lemon wedges for serving (optional)

Instructions:

Preheat your grill to medium-high heat.

In a large bowl, toss the quartered bell peppers, sliced zucchini, sliced yellow squash, and sliced red onion with olive oil, salt, and pepper until evenly coated. Place the vegetables on the preheated grill and cook for about 4-5 minutes per side, or until they are tender and have grill marks. Remove from the grill and set aside.

While the vegetables are grilling, prepare the quinoa. In a medium saucepan, combine the quinoa, water or vegetable broth, and salt. Bring to a boil, then reduce the heat to low, cover, and simmer for 15-20 minutes, or until the quinoa is cooked and the liquid is absorbed. Remove from heat and let it sit covered for 5 minutes. Fluff with a fork and let it cool slightly.

In a small bowl, whisk together the olive oil, balsamic vinegar, Dijon mustard, minced garlic, salt, and pepper to make the salad dressing.

In a large mixing bowl, combine the cooked quinoa, grilled vegetables, halved cherry tomatoes, and chopped basil leaves.

Pour the salad dressing over the quinoa and vegetables and toss gently to combine.

If using, sprinkle the crumbled feta cheese over the salad.

Serve the grilled vegetable and quinoa salad warm or at room temperature, garnished with lemon wedges if desired.

Enjoy your delicious and nutritious grilled vegetable and quinoa salad! It's packed with flavor and makes for a satisfying meal on its own or as a side dish.

Low-Sodium Beef and Barley Soup

Ingredients:

- 1 lb (450g) lean beef stew meat, cut into bite-sized pieces
- 1 tablespoon olive oil
- 1 onion, diced
- 2 carrots, diced
- 2 celery stalks, diced
- 2 cloves garlic, minced
- 1 teaspoon dried thyme
- 1 teaspoon dried rosemary
- 1/2 teaspoon black pepper
- 1/2 cup pearl barley
- 6 cups low-sodium beef broth
- 2 cups water
- 2 bay leaves
- Salt to taste
- Chopped fresh parsley for garnish (optional)

Instructions:

Heat the olive oil in a large pot or Dutch oven over medium heat. Add the diced onion, carrots, and celery. Cook, stirring occasionally, until the vegetables are softened, about 5-7 minutes.

Add the minced garlic, dried thyme, dried rosemary, and black pepper to the pot. Cook for another minute until fragrant.

Add the beef stew meat to the pot and cook until browned on all sides, about 5 minutes.

Stir in the pearl barley, low-sodium beef broth, water, and bay leaves.

Bring the soup to a boil, then reduce the heat to low and let it simmer, covered, for about 1 hour, or until the beef is tender and the barley is cooked through. Stir occasionally.

Once the soup is cooked, taste and adjust the seasoning with salt as needed. Remember, since this is a low-sodium recipe, you may not need much salt, if any. Once done, remove the bay leaves from the soup.

Ladle the low-sodium beef and barley soup into bowls and garnish with chopped fresh parsley, if desired.

Serve the soup hot with crusty bread or crackers on the side.

Enjoy your hearty and nutritious low-sodium beef and barley soup! It's perfect for a comforting meal, especially on a chilly day.

Lemon Herb Baked Cod

Ingredients:

- 4 cod fillets (about 6 ounces each)
- 2 tablespoons olive oil
- 2 tablespoons lemon juice
- Zest of 1 lemon
- 2 cloves garlic, minced
- 1 teaspoon chopped fresh thyme
- 1 teaspoon chopped fresh parsley
- Salt and pepper to taste
- Lemon slices for garnish (optional)
- Fresh parsley for garnish (optional)

Instructions:

Preheat your oven to 400°F (200°C). Line a baking dish with parchment paper or lightly grease it with olive oil.
Place the cod fillets in the prepared baking dish in a single layer.
In a small bowl, whisk together the olive oil, lemon juice, lemon zest, minced garlic, chopped thyme, chopped parsley, salt, and pepper.
Pour the lemon herb mixture over the cod fillets, ensuring they are evenly coated.
Place lemon slices on top of each cod fillet for extra flavor if desired.
Bake the cod in the preheated oven for 12-15 minutes, or until the fish is opaque and flakes easily with a fork.
Once done, remove the baked cod from the oven and let it rest for a few minutes.
Garnish the lemon herb baked cod with fresh parsley, if desired.
Serve hot with your favorite side dishes, such as steamed vegetables, rice, or roasted potatoes.

Enjoy your flavorful and tender lemon herb baked cod! It's a light and healthy dish that's perfect for a quick and easy dinner.

Turkey and Quinoa Stuffed Bell Peppers

Ingredients:

- 4 large bell peppers (any color), halved and seeds removed
- 1 tablespoon olive oil
- 1 onion, diced
- 2 cloves garlic, minced
- 1 lb (450g) lean ground turkey
- 1 cup cooked quinoa
- 1 can (14.5 ounces) diced tomatoes, drained
- 1 teaspoon dried oregano
- 1 teaspoon dried basil
- 1/2 teaspoon paprika
- Salt and pepper to taste
- 1 cup shredded mozzarella cheese
- Chopped fresh parsley for garnish (optional)

Instructions:

Preheat your oven to 375°F (190°C). Arrange the halved bell peppers in a baking dish, cut side up.
In a large skillet, heat the olive oil over medium heat. Add the diced onion and cook until softened, about 5 minutes.
Add the minced garlic to the skillet and cook for another minute until fragrant.
Add the ground turkey to the skillet and cook until browned, breaking it apart with a spoon as it cooks.
Stir in the cooked quinoa, diced tomatoes, dried oregano, dried basil, paprika, salt, and pepper. Cook for a few minutes until heated through and well combined.
Spoon the turkey and quinoa mixture into each halved bell pepper, filling them to the top.
Sprinkle the shredded mozzarella cheese evenly over the stuffed bell peppers.
Cover the baking dish with aluminum foil and bake in the preheated oven for about 25-30 minutes, or until the peppers are tender and the cheese is melted and bubbly.
Once done, remove the foil and broil for an additional 2-3 minutes to brown the cheese, if desired.

Remove the stuffed bell peppers from the oven and let them cool for a few minutes.
Garnish with chopped fresh parsley, if using, and serve hot.

Enjoy your delicious turkey and quinoa stuffed bell peppers! They make for a satisfying and nutritious meal that's packed with protein and flavor.

Baked Chicken Parmesan

Ingredients:

- 4 boneless, skinless chicken breasts
- Salt and pepper to taste
- 1 cup breadcrumbs (panko or regular)
- 1/2 cup grated Parmesan cheese
- 1 teaspoon dried Italian seasoning
- 2 eggs, beaten
- 1 cup marinara sauce
- 1 cup shredded mozzarella cheese
- Fresh basil leaves for garnish (optional)

Instructions:

Preheat your oven to 400°F (200°C). Lightly grease a baking dish with olive oil or cooking spray.
Season both sides of the chicken breasts with salt and pepper.
In a shallow dish, combine the breadcrumbs, grated Parmesan cheese, and dried Italian seasoning.
Dip each chicken breast into the beaten eggs, then dredge them in the breadcrumb mixture, pressing lightly to adhere the breadcrumbs to the chicken.
Place the coated chicken breasts in the prepared baking dish.
Bake the chicken breasts in the preheated oven for about 20-25 minutes, or until they are cooked through and the breadcrumbs are golden brown.
Once the chicken is cooked, remove the baking dish from the oven and spoon marinara sauce over each chicken breast.
Sprinkle shredded mozzarella cheese evenly over the marinara sauce.
Return the baking dish to the oven and bake for an additional 5-7 minutes, or until the cheese is melted and bubbly.
Once done, remove the baked chicken parmesan from the oven and let it cool for a few minutes.
Garnish with fresh basil leaves, if desired, and serve hot.

Enjoy your delicious baked chicken parmesan! Serve it with pasta or a side salad for a complete meal.

Roasted Asparagus with Lemon Zest

Ingredients:

- 1 lb (450g) fresh asparagus spears, trimmed
- 2 tablespoons olive oil
- Salt and pepper to taste
- Zest of 1 lemon
- Lemon wedges for serving (optional)

Instructions:

Preheat your oven to 425°F (220°C). Line a baking sheet with parchment paper or aluminum foil for easy cleanup.
Place the trimmed asparagus spears on the prepared baking sheet.
Drizzle the asparagus with olive oil and sprinkle with salt and pepper to taste. Toss to coat evenly.
Spread the asparagus out in a single layer on the baking sheet.
Roast the asparagus in the preheated oven for about 10-12 minutes, or until tender and lightly browned, shaking the pan halfway through cooking to ensure even roasting.
Once the asparagus is done roasting, remove it from the oven and transfer it to a serving platter.
Sprinkle the roasted asparagus with lemon zest, evenly distributing it over the spears.
Serve the roasted asparagus with lemon zest hot, with lemon wedges on the side for squeezing over the asparagus if desired.

Enjoy your delicious roasted asparagus with lemon zest! It's a vibrant and flavorful side dish that's perfect for any occasion.

Low-Sodium Chicken Fajitas

Ingredients:

- 1 lb (450g) boneless, skinless chicken breasts, thinly sliced
- 2 bell peppers (any color), thinly sliced
- 1 onion, thinly sliced
- 2 cloves garlic, minced
- 2 tablespoons olive oil
- 1 teaspoon chili powder
- 1/2 teaspoon ground cumin
- 1/2 teaspoon paprika
- 1/2 teaspoon garlic powder
- 1/4 teaspoon cayenne pepper (optional, for heat)
- Salt-free fajita seasoning blend (store-bought or homemade)
- Salt and pepper to taste
- Whole wheat or corn tortillas, for serving
- Optional toppings: salsa, guacamole, sour cream, shredded cheese, chopped cilantro, lime wedges

Instructions:

In a small bowl, combine the chili powder, ground cumin, paprika, garlic powder, cayenne pepper (if using), and salt-free fajita seasoning blend to make the seasoning mix.

Season the thinly sliced chicken breasts with half of the seasoning mix, tossing to coat evenly.

Heat 1 tablespoon of olive oil in a large skillet or cast-iron pan over medium-high heat. Add the seasoned chicken slices to the skillet and cook for about 5-7 minutes, stirring occasionally, until the chicken is cooked through and lightly browned. Remove the chicken from the skillet and set it aside on a plate.

In the same skillet, heat the remaining tablespoon of olive oil over medium-high heat. Add the thinly sliced bell peppers, sliced onion, and minced garlic to the skillet. Cook for about 5-7 minutes, stirring occasionally, until the vegetables are tender-crisp and slightly charred.

Return the cooked chicken to the skillet with the cooked vegetables. Sprinkle the remaining seasoning mix over the chicken and vegetables, tossing to coat evenly. Cook for another 2-3 minutes to heat through.

Taste and adjust the seasoning with salt and pepper if needed.
Once done, remove the skillet from the heat.
Serve the low-sodium chicken fajitas hot with whole wheat or corn tortillas and your favorite toppings such as salsa, guacamole, sour cream, shredded cheese, chopped cilantro, and lime wedges.

Enjoy your delicious and flavorful low-sodium chicken fajitas! They're perfect for a quick and satisfying meal any day of the week.

Herb-Marinated Grilled Steak

Ingredients:

- 4 steaks of your choice (such as ribeye, sirloin, or New York strip)
- 1/4 cup olive oil
- 2 cloves garlic, minced
- 2 tablespoons chopped fresh herbs (such as rosemary, thyme, and parsley)
- 2 tablespoons balsamic vinegar
- 1 tablespoon Worcestershire sauce
- 1 teaspoon Dijon mustard
- Salt and pepper to taste

Instructions:

In a small bowl, whisk together the olive oil, minced garlic, chopped fresh herbs, balsamic vinegar, Worcestershire sauce, Dijon mustard, salt, and pepper to make the marinade.

Place the steaks in a shallow dish or a large resealable plastic bag.

Pour the marinade over the steaks, making sure they are evenly coated. Massage the marinade into the steaks to ensure they are well coated.

Cover the dish or seal the bag and refrigerate for at least 30 minutes, or up to 4 hours, to allow the flavors to meld and the steaks to marinate.

Preheat your grill to medium-high heat.

Remove the steaks from the marinade and discard any excess marinade.

Grill the steaks on the preheated grill for about 4-6 minutes per side, depending on the thickness of the steaks and your desired level of doneness. For medium-rare, aim for an internal temperature of 130-135°F (54-57°C) on an instant-read meat thermometer inserted into the thickest part of the steak.

Once done, remove the steaks from the grill and let them rest for a few minutes before serving.

Serve the herb-marinated grilled steaks hot, garnished with additional chopped fresh herbs if desired.

Enjoy your flavorful and juicy herb-marinated grilled steaks! They pair well with a variety of side dishes, such as grilled vegetables, potatoes, or a fresh salad.

Lemon Herb Roasted Turkey Breast

Ingredients:

- 1 bone-in, skin-on turkey breast (about 4-5 pounds)
- 1/4 cup olive oil
- Zest of 1 lemon
- Juice of 1 lemon
- 2 cloves garlic, minced
- 1 tablespoon chopped fresh rosemary
- 1 tablespoon chopped fresh thyme
- 1 tablespoon chopped fresh parsley
- 1 teaspoon dried oregano
- 1 teaspoon dried sage
- Salt and pepper to taste
- Lemon slices for garnish (optional)
- Fresh herbs for garnish (optional)

Instructions:

Preheat your oven to 325°F (160°C). Place a roasting rack in a roasting pan.
Rinse the turkey breast under cold water and pat it dry with paper towels. Place the turkey breast on the roasting rack, breast side up.
In a small bowl, whisk together the olive oil, lemon zest, lemon juice, minced garlic, chopped fresh rosemary, thyme, parsley, oregano, sage, salt, and pepper to make the herb marinade.
Brush the herb marinade all over the turkey breast, making sure to coat it evenly.
Tuck the wing tips under the breast and tie the legs together with kitchen twine, if desired, to help the turkey cook evenly.
If using, place lemon slices on top of the turkey breast for extra flavor.
Roast the turkey breast in the preheated oven for about 1 1/2 to 2 hours, or until the internal temperature reaches 165°F (75°C) when tested with a meat thermometer inserted into the thickest part of the breast.
Once done, remove the turkey breast from the oven and let it rest for about 15-20 minutes before carving.
Carve the turkey breast into slices and arrange them on a serving platter.
Garnish the lemon herb roasted turkey breast with fresh herbs, if desired, and serve hot.

Enjoy your delicious and aromatic lemon herb roasted turkey breast! It's sure to be a hit at your dinner table, whether for a special occasion or a family meal.

Low-Sodium Lentil Soup

Ingredients:

- 1 cup dried lentils, rinsed and drained
- 6 cups low-sodium vegetable broth or chicken broth
- 1 onion, diced
- 2 carrots, diced
- 2 celery stalks, diced
- 2 cloves garlic, minced
- 1 teaspoon olive oil
- 1 bay leaf
- 1 teaspoon dried thyme
- 1 teaspoon dried oregano
- 1/2 teaspoon ground cumin
- Salt-free seasoning blend (optional)
- Salt and pepper to taste
- Fresh parsley or cilantro for garnish (optional)
- Lemon wedges for serving (optional)

Instructions:

Heat the olive oil in a large pot over medium heat. Add the diced onion, carrots, and celery. Cook, stirring occasionally, until the vegetables are softened, about 5-7 minutes.

Add the minced garlic to the pot and cook for another minute until fragrant.

Add the rinsed and drained lentils, low-sodium vegetable broth or chicken broth, bay leaf, dried thyme, dried oregano, and ground cumin to the pot. Stir to combine.

Bring the soup to a boil, then reduce the heat to low and let it simmer, partially covered, for about 20-25 minutes, or until the lentils are tender.

Taste the soup and adjust the seasoning with salt and pepper as needed. You can also add salt-free seasoning blend for extra flavor, if desired.

Once the lentils are tender, remove the bay leaf from the soup.

If you prefer a smoother texture, you can blend a portion of the soup using an immersion blender or transfer a portion to a blender and puree until smooth, then return it to the pot.

Serve the low-sodium lentil soup hot, garnished with fresh parsley or cilantro if desired, and with lemon wedges on the side for squeezing over the soup.

Enjoy your flavorful and nutritious low-sodium lentil soup! It's a comforting and satisfying meal that's perfect for lunch or dinner.

Grilled Lemon Garlic Shrimp Skewers

Ingredients:

- 1 lb (450g) large shrimp, peeled and deveined
- 3 cloves garlic, minced
- Zest of 1 lemon
- Juice of 1 lemon
- 2 tablespoons olive oil
- 1 tablespoon chopped fresh parsley
- Salt and pepper to taste
- Wooden or metal skewers

Instructions:

If you're using wooden skewers, soak them in water for at least 30 minutes to prevent them from burning on the grill.
In a small bowl, whisk together the minced garlic, lemon zest, lemon juice, olive oil, chopped fresh parsley, salt, and pepper to make the marinade.
Place the peeled and deveined shrimp in a shallow dish or a large resealable plastic bag.
Pour the marinade over the shrimp, making sure they are evenly coated. Toss to coat the shrimp evenly.
Cover the dish or seal the bag and refrigerate for at least 30 minutes, or up to 1 hour, to allow the flavors to meld and the shrimp to marinate.
Preheat your grill to medium-high heat.
Thread the marinated shrimp onto the skewers, dividing them evenly among the skewers.
Once the grill is hot, place the shrimp skewers on the grill and cook for about 2-3 minutes per side, or until the shrimp are pink and opaque, and lightly charred.
Once done, remove the shrimp skewers from the grill and transfer them to a serving platter.
Serve the grilled lemon garlic shrimp skewers hot, garnished with additional chopped fresh parsley if desired.

Enjoy your flavorful and aromatic grilled lemon garlic shrimp skewers! They make for a delicious appetizer or main dish at any summer gathering.

Roasted Cauliflower with Garlic and Herbs

Ingredients:

- 1 head cauliflower, cut into florets
- 3 cloves garlic, minced
- 2 tablespoons olive oil
- 1 teaspoon dried thyme
- 1 teaspoon dried rosemary
- 1/2 teaspoon dried oregano
- Salt and pepper to taste
- Fresh parsley for garnish (optional)
- Lemon wedges for serving (optional)

Instructions:

Preheat your oven to 425°F (220°C). Line a baking sheet with parchment paper or aluminum foil for easy cleanup.

In a large bowl, toss the cauliflower florets with minced garlic, olive oil, dried thyme, dried rosemary, dried oregano, salt, and pepper until evenly coated.

Spread the seasoned cauliflower out in a single layer on the prepared baking sheet.

Roast the cauliflower in the preheated oven for about 25-30 minutes, or until golden brown and tender, stirring halfway through the cooking time for even browning.

Once the cauliflower is roasted to your liking, remove it from the oven and transfer it to a serving dish.

Garnish the roasted cauliflower with fresh parsley, if desired, and serve hot.

Serve the roasted cauliflower with garlic and herbs hot, with lemon wedges on the side for squeezing over the cauliflower if desired.

Enjoy your delicious and flavorful roasted cauliflower with garlic and herbs! It's a perfect side dish for any meal and pairs well with a variety of main dishes.

Low-Sodium Vegetable and Bean Chili

Ingredients:

- 1 tablespoon olive oil
- 1 onion, diced
- 2 cloves garlic, minced
- 2 carrots, diced
- 2 celery stalks, diced
- 1 bell pepper (any color), diced
- 1 zucchini, diced
- 1 yellow squash, diced
- 1 can (14.5 ounces) low-sodium diced tomatoes
- 1 can (15 ounces) low-sodium black beans, drained and rinsed
- 1 can (15 ounces) low-sodium kidney beans, drained and rinsed
- 2 cups low-sodium vegetable broth
- 2 tablespoons tomato paste
- 1 tablespoon chili powder
- 1 teaspoon ground cumin
- 1 teaspoon dried oregano
- 1/2 teaspoon smoked paprika
- Salt and pepper to taste
- Optional toppings: chopped fresh cilantro, avocado slices, shredded cheese, sour cream, lime wedges

Instructions:

Heat the olive oil in a large pot over medium heat. Add the diced onion and cook until softened, about 5 minutes.

Add the minced garlic to the pot and cook for another minute until fragrant.

Add the diced carrots, celery, bell pepper, zucchini, and yellow squash to the pot. Cook, stirring occasionally, for about 5-7 minutes, or until the vegetables are softened.

Stir in the low-sodium diced tomatoes, drained and rinsed black beans, drained and rinsed kidney beans, low-sodium vegetable broth, tomato paste, chili powder, ground cumin, dried oregano, smoked paprika, salt, and pepper.

Bring the chili to a boil, then reduce the heat to low and let it simmer, uncovered, for about 20-25 minutes, stirring occasionally, to allow the flavors to meld and the chili to thicken.

Taste the chili and adjust the seasoning with salt and pepper as needed.

Once the chili is done simmering and the vegetables are tender, remove it from the heat.

Serve the low-sodium vegetable and bean chili hot, garnished with your favorite toppings such as chopped fresh cilantro, avocado slices, shredded cheese, sour cream, and lime wedges.

Enjoy your flavorful and nutritious low-sodium vegetable and bean chili! It's perfect for a cozy meal on a chilly day.

Baked Lemon Herb Tilapia

Ingredients:

- 4 tilapia fillets (about 6 ounces each)
- 2 tablespoons olive oil
- Zest of 1 lemon
- Juice of 1 lemon
- 2 cloves garlic, minced
- 1 tablespoon chopped fresh parsley
- 1 tablespoon chopped fresh dill
- Salt and pepper to taste
- Lemon slices for garnish (optional)
- Fresh parsley for garnish (optional)

Instructions:

Preheat your oven to 400°F (200°C). Line a baking dish with parchment paper or aluminum foil for easy cleanup.
Place the tilapia fillets in the prepared baking dish in a single layer.
In a small bowl, whisk together the olive oil, lemon zest, lemon juice, minced garlic, chopped fresh parsley, chopped fresh dill, salt, and pepper to make the herb marinade.
Pour the herb marinade over the tilapia fillets, making sure they are evenly coated.
If desired, place lemon slices on top of each tilapia fillet for extra flavor.
Bake the tilapia in the preheated oven for about 12-15 minutes, or until the fish is opaque and flakes easily with a fork.
Once done, remove the baked tilapia from the oven and let it rest for a few minutes.
Garnish the baked lemon herb tilapia with fresh parsley, if desired.
Serve hot with your favorite side dishes, such as steamed vegetables, rice, or a fresh salad.

Enjoy your delicious and flavorful baked lemon herb tilapia! It's a light and healthy dish that's perfect for a quick and easy dinner.

Turkey and Vegetable Skillet

Ingredients:

- 1 lb (450g) ground turkey
- 1 onion, diced
- 2 cloves garlic, minced
- 2 bell peppers (any color), diced
- 2 medium zucchini, diced
- 1 cup cherry tomatoes, halved
- 1 teaspoon dried oregano
- 1 teaspoon dried basil
- Salt and pepper to taste
- 2 tablespoons olive oil
- Grated Parmesan cheese for garnish (optional)
- Fresh parsley for garnish (optional)

Instructions:

Heat olive oil in a large skillet over medium heat.
Add diced onion and minced garlic to the skillet. Cook until softened and fragrant, about 3-4 minutes.
Add ground turkey to the skillet, breaking it apart with a spoon. Cook until the turkey is browned and cooked through, about 5-7 minutes.
Once the turkey is cooked, add diced bell peppers and diced zucchini to the skillet. Cook until the vegetables are tender, about 5 minutes.
Stir in halved cherry tomatoes, dried oregano, dried basil, salt, and pepper. Cook for an additional 2-3 minutes until the tomatoes are heated through.
Taste and adjust seasoning if needed.
Once done, remove the skillet from heat.
Garnish the turkey and vegetable skillet with grated Parmesan cheese and fresh parsley, if desired.
Serve hot as is, or over cooked rice, quinoa, or pasta.

Enjoy your delicious and nutritious turkey and vegetable skillet! It's a quick and easy meal that's perfect for a busy weeknight.

Herb-Roasted Chicken Thighs

Ingredients:

- 6 bone-in, skin-on chicken thighs
- 2 tablespoons olive oil
- 2 cloves garlic, minced
- 1 tablespoon chopped fresh rosemary
- 1 tablespoon chopped fresh thyme
- 1 tablespoon chopped fresh parsley
- 1 teaspoon dried oregano
- Salt and pepper to taste
- Lemon wedges for serving (optional)
- Fresh herbs for garnish (optional)

Instructions:

Preheat your oven to 400°F (200°C). Line a baking sheet with parchment paper or aluminum foil for easy cleanup.
In a small bowl, mix together the olive oil, minced garlic, chopped fresh rosemary, chopped fresh thyme, chopped fresh parsley, dried oregano, salt, and pepper to make the herb marinade.
Pat the chicken thighs dry with paper towels. Place them on the prepared baking sheet, skin side up.
Brush the herb marinade all over the chicken thighs, making sure they are evenly coated.
Once the chicken thighs are coated with the herb marinade, place them in the preheated oven.
Roast the chicken thighs in the oven for about 30-35 minutes, or until the internal temperature reaches 165°F (75°C) when tested with a meat thermometer inserted into the thickest part of the thigh.
Once done, remove the chicken thighs from the oven and let them rest for a few minutes.
Serve the herb-roasted chicken thighs hot, garnished with fresh herbs and lemon wedges if desired.

Enjoy your delicious and flavorful herb-roasted chicken thighs! They're perfect for a comforting meal any day of the week.

Lemon Garlic Roasted Salmon

Ingredients:

- 4 salmon fillets (about 6 ounces each), skin-on or skinless
- 2 tablespoons olive oil
- 4 cloves garlic, minced
- Zest of 1 lemon
- Juice of 1 lemon
- 1 tablespoon chopped fresh parsley
- Salt and pepper to taste
- Lemon slices for garnish (optional)
- Fresh parsley for garnish (optional)

Instructions:

Preheat your oven to 400°F (200°C). Line a baking sheet with parchment paper or aluminum foil for easy cleanup.

Place the salmon fillets on the prepared baking sheet, skin side down if using skin-on fillets.

In a small bowl, whisk together the olive oil, minced garlic, lemon zest, lemon juice, chopped fresh parsley, salt, and pepper to make the lemon garlic marinade.

Pour the lemon garlic marinade over the salmon fillets, making sure they are evenly coated.

Once the salmon fillets are coated with the marinade, place them in the preheated oven.

Roast the salmon in the oven for about 12-15 minutes, depending on the thickness of the fillets, or until the salmon is cooked through and flakes easily with a fork.

Once done, remove the salmon from the oven and let it rest for a few minutes. Serve the lemon garlic roasted salmon hot, garnished with lemon slices and fresh parsley if desired.

Enjoy your delicious and flavorful lemon garlic roasted salmon! It's a healthy and satisfying dish that's perfect for a quick and easy dinner.

Low-Sodium Beef and Broccoli Stir-Fry

Ingredients:

- 1 lb (450g) flank steak, thinly sliced against the grain
- 2 tablespoons low-sodium soy sauce
- 1 tablespoon rice vinegar
- 1 tablespoon cornstarch
- 2 tablespoons olive oil, divided
- 3 cloves garlic, minced
- 1 teaspoon minced ginger
- 1 head broccoli, cut into florets
- 1 red bell pepper, thinly sliced
- 1/2 cup low-sodium beef broth
- 1 tablespoon hoisin sauce
- Sesame seeds for garnish (optional)
- Cooked rice or noodles, for serving

Instructions:

In a bowl, combine the sliced flank steak with low-sodium soy sauce, rice vinegar, and cornstarch. Let it marinate for about 15-20 minutes.

Heat 1 tablespoon of olive oil in a large skillet or wok over medium-high heat.

Add the minced garlic and ginger, and cook for about 30 seconds until fragrant.

Add the marinated flank steak to the skillet in a single layer. Cook for 2-3 minutes without stirring to allow the steak to sear and brown on one side. Then, stir-fry for an additional 2-3 minutes until the steak is cooked through. Remove the steak from the skillet and set aside.

In the same skillet, add the remaining tablespoon of olive oil. Add the broccoli florets and sliced red bell pepper. Stir-fry for about 3-4 minutes until the vegetables are tender-crisp.

In a small bowl, mix together low-sodium beef broth and hoisin sauce. Pour the mixture into the skillet with the vegetables.

Return the cooked steak to the skillet with the vegetables. Stir everything together and cook for an additional 1-2 minutes until the sauce thickens slightly and coats the beef and vegetables.

Taste and adjust seasoning if needed. If desired, sprinkle sesame seeds on top for garnish.

Serve the low-sodium beef and broccoli stir-fry hot over cooked rice or noodles.

Enjoy your delicious and flavorful low-sodium beef and broccoli stir-fry! It's a nutritious and satisfying meal that's perfect for a quick and easy dinner.

Quinoa Salad with Lemon Herb Vinaigrette

Ingredients for the Salad:

- 1 cup quinoa, rinsed
- 2 cups water or vegetable broth
- 1 cucumber, diced
- 1 bell pepper (any color), diced
- 1 cup cherry tomatoes, halved
- 1/4 cup red onion, finely chopped
- 1/4 cup chopped fresh parsley
- 1/4 cup chopped fresh mint
- Salt and pepper to taste

Ingredients for the Lemon Herb Vinaigrette:

- 1/4 cup olive oil
- Zest of 1 lemon
- Juice of 1 lemon
- 2 tablespoons red wine vinegar
- 1 tablespoon honey or maple syrup (optional)
- 1 clove garlic, minced
- 1 teaspoon Dijon mustard
- 1 tablespoon chopped fresh parsley
- 1 tablespoon chopped fresh mint
- Salt and pepper to taste

Instructions:

In a medium saucepan, combine the quinoa and water or vegetable broth. Bring to a boil, then reduce the heat to low, cover, and simmer for 15-20 minutes, or until the quinoa is cooked and the liquid is absorbed. Remove from heat and let it cool.

In a large mixing bowl, combine the cooked and cooled quinoa with diced cucumber, diced bell pepper, halved cherry tomatoes, finely chopped red onion, chopped fresh parsley, and chopped fresh mint. Season with salt and pepper to taste.

In a small bowl or jar, whisk together the olive oil, lemon zest, lemon juice, red wine vinegar, honey or maple syrup (if using), minced garlic, Dijon mustard,

chopped fresh parsley, and chopped fresh mint to make the lemon herb vinaigrette. Season with salt and pepper to taste.
Pour the lemon herb vinaigrette over the quinoa salad and toss to coat evenly. Taste and adjust seasoning if needed. Add more lemon juice or vinegar for extra tang, or honey or maple syrup for sweetness.
Serve the quinoa salad with lemon herb vinaigrette chilled or at room temperature.

Enjoy your refreshing and flavorful quinoa salad with lemon herb vinaigrette! It's perfect for picnics, potlucks, or as a light and healthy lunch or side dish.

Grilled Vegetable and Hummus Wrap

Ingredients:

- 4 large whole wheat tortillas or wraps
- 1 zucchini, sliced lengthwise
- 1 yellow squash, sliced lengthwise
- 1 red bell pepper, sliced into strips
- 1 yellow bell pepper, sliced into strips
- 1 red onion, sliced into rings
- 1 cup cherry tomatoes
- 2 tablespoons olive oil
- Salt and pepper to taste
- 1 cup hummus (store-bought or homemade)
- Fresh spinach or lettuce leaves
- Optional: crumbled feta cheese, chopped fresh herbs (such as parsley or basil)

Instructions:

Preheat your grill to medium-high heat.
In a large bowl, toss the sliced zucchini, yellow squash, bell peppers, red onion, and cherry tomatoes with olive oil, salt, and pepper until evenly coated.
Place the vegetables on the preheated grill. Cook for about 3-5 minutes per side, or until they are tender and slightly charred.
Once the vegetables are grilled to your liking, remove them from the grill and let them cool slightly.
Warm the tortillas or wraps slightly on the grill or in a microwave for a few seconds to make them more pliable.
Spread a generous layer of hummus onto each tortilla or wrap.
Top each tortilla with a handful of fresh spinach or lettuce leaves.
Arrange the grilled vegetables on top of the spinach or lettuce leaves.
If desired, sprinkle crumbled feta cheese and chopped fresh herbs over the grilled vegetables.
Roll up the tortillas tightly into wraps.
Slice the wraps in half diagonally and serve immediately.

Enjoy your delicious and nutritious grilled vegetable and hummus wraps! They make for a satisfying and flavorful meal that's perfect for lunch or a light dinner.

Low-Sodium Chicken and Rice Casserole

Ingredients:

- 1 lb (450g) boneless, skinless chicken breasts, diced
- 1 cup uncooked white or brown rice
- 2 cups low-sodium chicken broth
- 1 cup diced carrots
- 1 cup frozen peas
- 1 small onion, diced
- 2 cloves garlic, minced
- 1 tablespoon olive oil
- 1 teaspoon dried thyme
- 1 teaspoon dried parsley
- 1/2 teaspoon dried oregano
- Salt and pepper to taste
- 1 cup shredded low-sodium cheese (such as cheddar or mozzarella), optional

Instructions:

Preheat your oven to 375°F (190°C). Grease a 9x13-inch baking dish with non-stick cooking spray.

In a large skillet, heat the olive oil over medium heat. Add the diced chicken and cook until browned on all sides, about 5-7 minutes. Remove the chicken from the skillet and set aside.

In the same skillet, add the diced onion and minced garlic. Cook until softened and fragrant, about 3-4 minutes.

Add the uncooked rice, diced carrots, frozen peas, dried thyme, dried parsley, and dried oregano to the skillet. Stir to combine.

Pour the low-sodium chicken broth into the skillet and bring to a simmer. Let it cook for about 5 minutes, stirring occasionally.

Remove the skillet from the heat and stir in the cooked chicken. Season with salt and pepper to taste.

Transfer the chicken and rice mixture to the prepared baking dish and spread it out evenly.

Cover the baking dish with aluminum foil and bake in the preheated oven for 30 minutes.

Remove the foil from the baking dish and sprinkle the shredded low-sodium cheese over the top, if using.

Return the baking dish to the oven and bake, uncovered, for an additional 10-15 minutes, or until the cheese is melted and bubbly.

Once done, remove the casserole from the oven and let it cool for a few minutes before serving.

Enjoy your delicious and comforting low-sodium chicken and rice casserole! It's a wholesome and satisfying dish that's perfect for a family dinner.

Herb-Marinated Grilled Chicken Breast

Ingredients:

- 4 boneless, skinless chicken breasts
- 1/4 cup olive oil
- 2 tablespoons lemon juice
- 2 cloves garlic, minced
- 1 tablespoon chopped fresh parsley
- 1 tablespoon chopped fresh basil
- 1 tablespoon chopped fresh rosemary
- 1 tablespoon chopped fresh thyme
- Salt and pepper to taste

Instructions:

In a small bowl, whisk together the olive oil, lemon juice, minced garlic, chopped fresh parsley, chopped fresh basil, chopped fresh rosemary, chopped fresh thyme, salt, and pepper to make the herb marinade.

Place the chicken breasts in a shallow dish or a large resealable plastic bag. Pour the herb marinade over the chicken breasts, making sure they are evenly coated. Massage the marinade into the chicken to ensure it's well coated.

Cover the dish or seal the bag and refrigerate for at least 30 minutes, or up to 4 hours, to allow the flavors to meld and the chicken to marinate.

Preheat your grill to medium-high heat.

Remove the chicken breasts from the marinade and discard any excess marinade.

Place the chicken breasts on the preheated grill. Grill for about 6-8 minutes per side, or until the internal temperature reaches 165°F (75°C) when tested with a meat thermometer inserted into the thickest part of the breast.

Once done, remove the chicken breasts from the grill and let them rest for a few minutes before serving.

Serve the herb-marinated grilled chicken breasts hot, garnished with additional chopped fresh herbs if desired.

Enjoy your flavorful and juicy herb-marinated grilled chicken breasts! They're perfect for a summertime barbecue or a quick and easy weeknight dinner.

Lemon Herb Baked Halibut

Ingredients:

- 4 halibut fillets (about 6 ounces each)
- 2 tablespoons olive oil
- 2 cloves garlic, minced
- Zest of 1 lemon
- Juice of 1 lemon
- 1 tablespoon chopped fresh parsley
- 1 tablespoon chopped fresh dill
- Salt and pepper, to taste
- Lemon slices, for garnish
- Fresh parsley, for garnish

Instructions:

Preheat your oven to 375°F (190°C). Grease a baking dish lightly with olive oil or non-stick cooking spray.
Rinse the halibut fillets under cold water and pat them dry with paper towels.
Place them in the prepared baking dish and set aside.
In a small bowl, whisk together the olive oil, minced garlic, lemon zest, lemon juice, chopped parsley, chopped dill, salt, and pepper.
Pour the herb mixture over the halibut fillets, making sure they are evenly coated.
Place lemon slices on top of each halibut fillet for extra flavor.
Bake the halibut in the preheated oven for about 15-20 minutes, or until the fish is cooked through and flakes easily with a fork.
Once done, remove the halibut from the oven and garnish with fresh parsley.
Serve hot with your favorite side dishes, such as roasted vegetables, rice, or a salad.

Enjoy your Lemon Herb Baked Halibut!

Low-Sodium Ratatouille

Ingredients:

- 1 medium eggplant, diced
- 2 medium zucchinis, diced
- 1 large red bell pepper, diced
- 1 large yellow bell pepper, diced
- 1 onion, diced
- 2 cloves garlic, minced
- 2 tablespoons olive oil
- 1 can (14 oz) low-sodium diced tomatoes
- 2 tablespoons tomato paste
- 1 teaspoon dried thyme
- 1 teaspoon dried oregano
- Salt substitute (e.g., potassium-based) to taste
- Freshly ground black pepper to taste
- Chopped fresh basil, for garnish

Instructions:

Preheat the oven to 375°F (190°C).

In a large skillet, heat the olive oil over medium heat. Add the diced onion and minced garlic, and sauté until softened, about 3-4 minutes.

Add the diced eggplant, zucchini, red bell pepper, and yellow bell pepper to the skillet. Cook, stirring occasionally, until the vegetables are slightly tender, about 5-7 minutes.

Stir in the low-sodium diced tomatoes, tomato paste, dried thyme, dried oregano, salt substitute, and black pepper. Cook for an additional 2-3 minutes, allowing the flavors to meld together.

Transfer the vegetable mixture to a baking dish or casserole dish, spreading it out evenly.

Cover the baking dish with aluminum foil and bake in the preheated oven for 25-30 minutes, or until the vegetables are fully tender.

Once done, remove the foil and garnish the ratatouille with chopped fresh basil. Serve hot as a side dish or as a main course with crusty bread or over cooked grains like quinoa or rice.

Enjoy your flavorful low-sodium ratatouille!

www.ingramcontent.com/pod-product-compliance
Lightning Source LLC
LaVergne TN
LVHW062048070526
838201LV00080B/2198